At Sylvan, we believe reading is one of life's most important and enriching abilities, and we're glad you've chosen our resources to help your child build this critically important skill. We know that the time you spend with your children reinforcing the lessons learned in school will contribute to their love of reading. This love of reading will translate into academic achievement. Successful readers are ready for the world around them, ready to do research, ready to experience the world of literature, and prepared to make the connections necessary to achieve in school and in life.

We use a research-based, step-by-step process in teaching reading at Sylvan that includes thought-provoking reading selections and activities. As students increase their success as readers, they become more confident. With increasing confidence, students build even more success. Our Page Per Day books are designed to help you to help your child build the skills and confidence that will contribute to your child's success in school.

Included with your purchase of this Page Per Day book is a coupon for a discount at a participating Sylvan Learning center. We hope you will use this coupon to further your child's academic journey. To learn more about Sylvan and our innovative in-center programs, call 1-800-EDUCATE or visit www.SylvanLearning.com.

We look forward to partnering with you to support the development of a confident, well-prepared, independent learner.

The Sylvan Team

Tips for Reading Success

Read to your child every day. This will help your child build a love of reading—and is a great opportunity to spend quality time together. Pick a variety of books, making sure to include books with rhymes.

Set aside 20 to 30 minutes a day. Be mindful of your child's attention span. Stop when your child is no longer engaged so that reading doesn't become a chore.

Read with expression. Instill the spirit of the story into your reading. This will also model appropriate reading for your child.

Reread your child's favorite stories. Indulge repeated requests for favorite stories or books. A desire to hear a story again is an indication that your child enjoys the benefits of reading.

Ask your child questions about the story. Before you start, look at the picture on the cover and talk about what might happen in the story. Stop now and then while reading to ask your child questions and encourage active participation.

Point out words during the day. Point out words that your child encounters every day. They may be on a cereal box or a traffic sign. This will encourage your child to see that reading can happen anywhere.

Go to the library. Help your child see the incredible world of books. Let your child pick out books that he or she finds appealing.

Pre-K Page Per Day:
Letters

Published in the United States by Random House, Inc., New York, and in Canada by Random House of Canada Limited, Toronto.

www.tutoring.sylvanlearning.com

Producer & Editorial Direction: The Linguistic Edge
Writer: Margaret Crocker
Cover and Interior Illustrations: Tim Goldman, Shawn Finley, and Duendes del Sur
Layout and Art Direction: SunDried Penguin

First Edition

ISBN: 978-0-307-94455-9
ISSN: 2161-9921

This book is available at special discounts for bulk purchases for sales promotions or premiums. For more information, write to Special Markets/Premium Sales, 1745 Broadway, MD 6-2, New York, New York 10019 or e-mail specialmarkets@randomhouse.com.

PRINTED IN THE USA

10 9 8 7

Trace & Sing

TRACE the letter **A**. START at the green arrow labeled with a number 1.

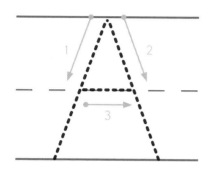

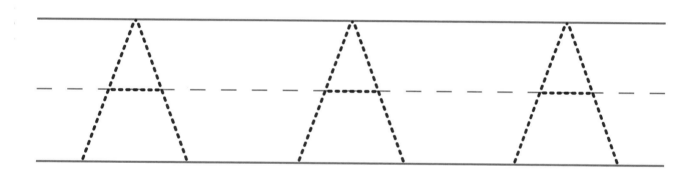

SING this song to the tune of *Wheels on the Bus*.

The letter of the day is

A-A-A, A-A-A, A-A-A!

The letter of the day is

A-A-A,

Today is letter A!

MAKE an **A** using three crayons (two long and one short).

The Letter B

Trace & Sing

TRACE the letter **B**. START at the green arrow labeled with a number 1.

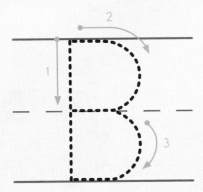

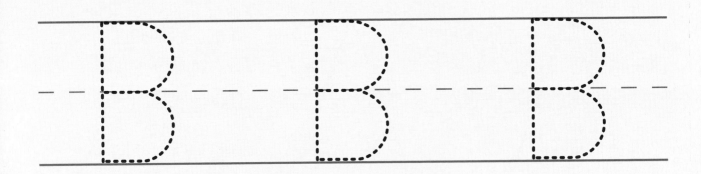

SING this song to the tune of *BINGO*.

We learn a letter every day.

Today it's letter **B**!

B, B, B-B-B!

B, B, B-B-B!

B, B, B-B-B!

And that's the letter **B**!

MAKE a **B** using beads.

Trace & Sing

TRACE the letter **C**. START at the green arrow labeled with a number 1.

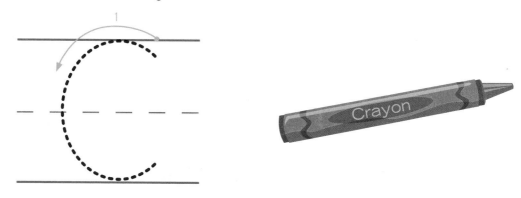

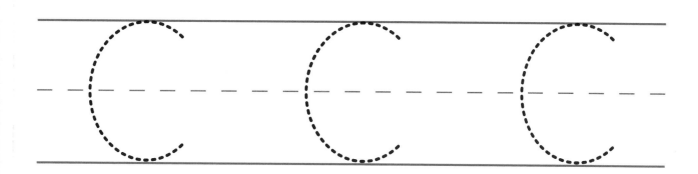

SING this song to the tune of *Wheels on the Bus*.

MAKE a **C** using your left hand.

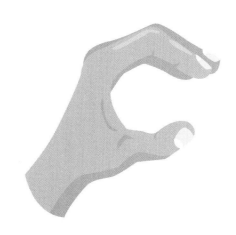

The letter of the day is

C-C-C, C-C-C, C-C-C!

The letter of the day is

C-C-C,

Today is letter **C**!

Trace & Sing

TRACE the letter **D**. START at the green arrow labeled with a number 1.

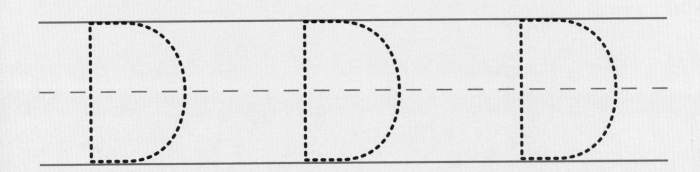

SING this song to the tune of *BINGO*.

MAKE a **D** using a pencil and string.

We learn a letter every day.

Today it's letter **D**!

D, D, D-D-D!

D, D, D-D-D!

D, D, D-D-D!

And that's the letter **D**!

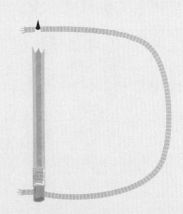

Trace & Sing

TRACE the letter **E**. START at the green arrow labeled with a number 1.

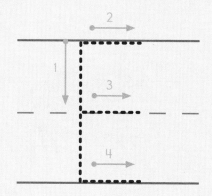

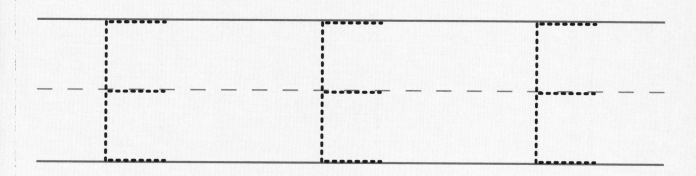

SING this song to the tune of *Wheels on the Bus*.

The letter of the day is

E-E-E, E-E-E, E-E-E!

The letter of the day is

E-E-E,

Today is letter E!

MAKE an **E** using four drinking straws (one long and three short).

Trace & Sing

TRACE the letter **F**. START at the green arrow labeled with a number 1.

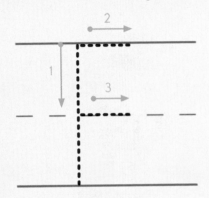

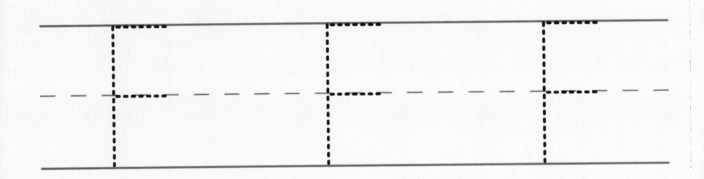

SING this song to the tune of *BINGO*.

MAKE an **F** using three sticks (one long and two short).

We learn a letter every day.

Today it's letter **F**!

F, F, F-F-F!

F, F, F-F-F!

F, F, F-F-F!

And that's the letter **F**!

Trace & Sing

TRACE the letter **G**. START at the green arrow labeled with a number 1.

SING this song to the tune of *Wheels on the Bus.*

MAKE a **G** using clay.

The letter of the day is
G-G-G, G-G-G, G-G-G!
The letter of the day is
G-G-G,
Today is letter **G!**

The Letter H

Trace & Sing

TRACE the letter **H**. START at the green arrow labeled with a number 1.

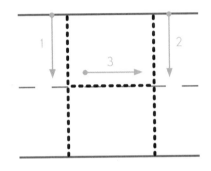

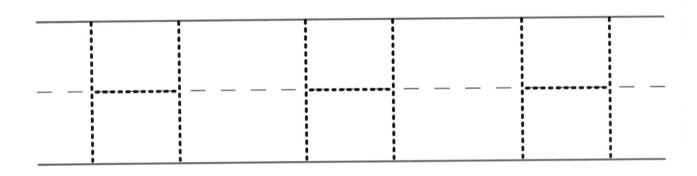

SING this song to the tune of *BINGO*.

We learn a letter every day.

Today it's letter **H**!

H, H, H-H-H!

H, H, H-H-H!

H, H, H-H-H!

And that's the letter **H**!

MAKE an **H** using blocks
(two long and one short).

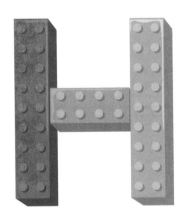

Trace & Sing

TRACE the letter **I**. START at the green arrow labeled with a number 1.

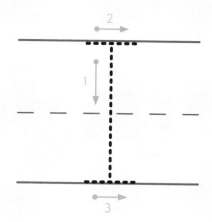

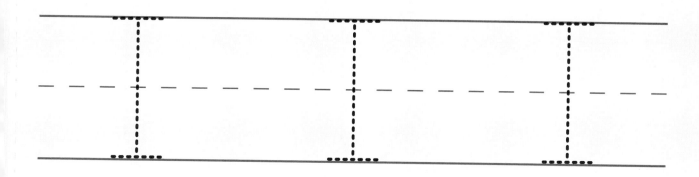

SING this song to the tune of *Wheels on the Bus.*

FIND three things that look like an **I**.

The letter of the day is

I-I-I, I-I-I, I-I-I!

The letter of the day is

I-I-I,

Today is letter **I**!

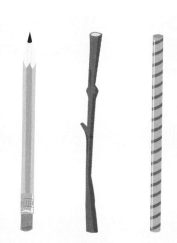

Trace & Sing

TRACE the letter **J**. START at the green arrow labeled with a number 1.

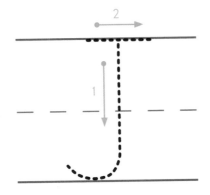

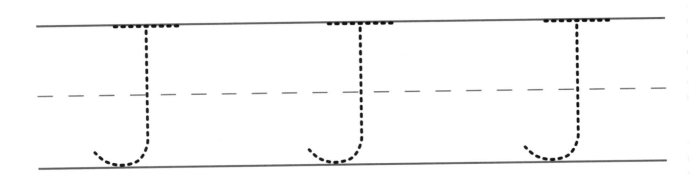

SING this song to the tune of *BINGO*.

We learn a letter every day.

Today it's letter **J**!

J, J, J-J-J!

J, J, J-J-J!

J, J, J-J-J!

And that's the letter **J**!

MAKE a **J** using a scarf.

Trace & Sing

TRACE the letter **K**. START at the green arrow labeled with a number 1.

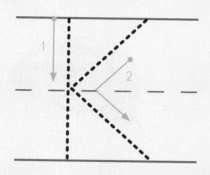

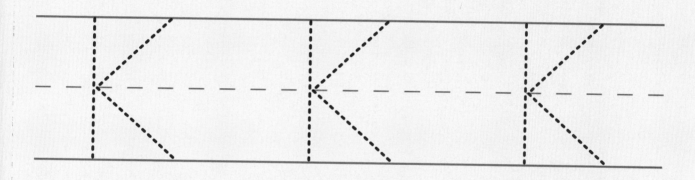

SING this song to the tune of *Wheels on the Bus.*

The letter of the day is

K-K-K, K-K-K, K-K-K!

The letter of the day is

K-K-K,

Today is letter K!

MAKE a **K** using green beans (one long and two short).

Trace & Sing

TRACE the letter **L**. START at the green arrow labeled with a number 1.

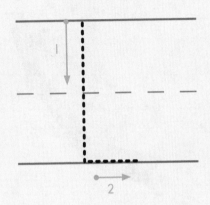

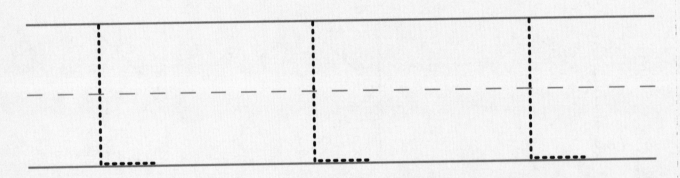

SING this song to the tune of *BINGO*.

MAKE an **L** using your left hand.

We learn a letter every day.

Today it's letter L!

L, L, L-L-L!

L, L, L-L-L!

L, L, L-L-L!

And that's the letter L!

Trace & Sing

TRACE the letter **M**. START at the green arrow labeled with a number 1.

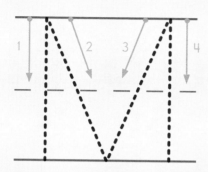

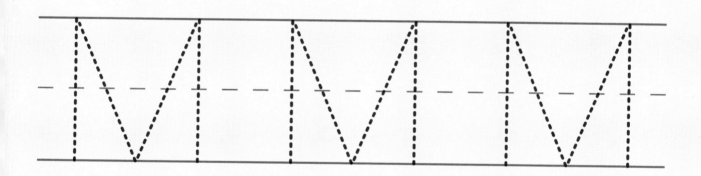

SING this song to the tune of *Wheels on the Bus.*

The letter of the day is

M-M-M, M-M-M, M-M-M!

The letter of the day is

M-M-M,

Today is letter **M**!

MAKE an **M** out of two pairs of pants.

Trace & Sing

TRACE the letter **N**. START at the green arrow labeled with a number 1.

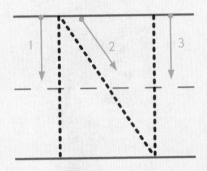

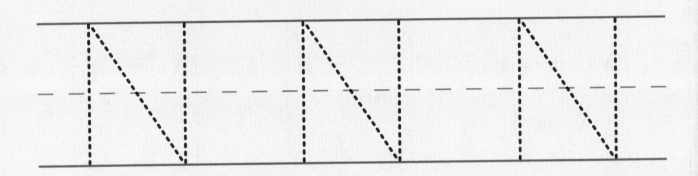

SING this song to the tune of *BINGO*.

We learn a letter every day.

Today it's letter **N**!

N, N, N-N-N!

N, N, N-N-N!

N, N, N-N-N!

And that's the letter **N**!

MAKE an **N** using three pencils.

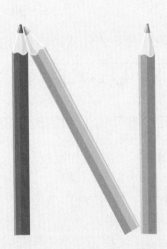

Trace & Sing

TRACE the letter O. START at the green arrow labeled with a number 1.

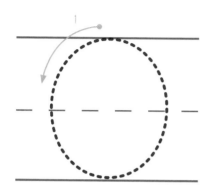

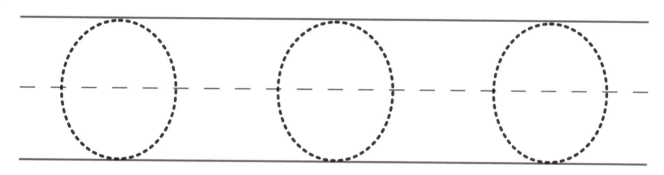

SING this song to the tune of
Wheels on the Bus.

The letter of the day is
O-O-O, O-O-O, O-O-O!
The letter of the day is
O-O-O,
Today is letter O!

FIND three things that look like an O.

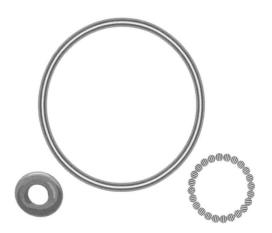

Trace & Sing

TRACE the letter **P**. START at the green arrow labeled with a number 1.

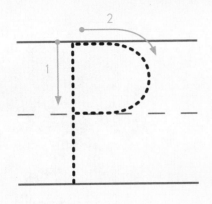

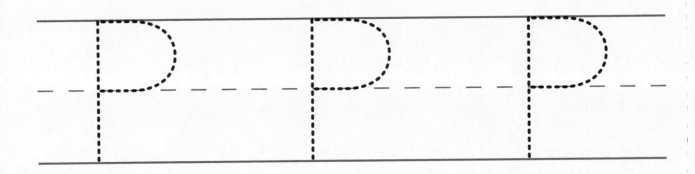

SING this song to the tune of *BINGO*.

We learn a letter every day.

Today it's letter **P**!

P, P, P-P-P!

P, P, P-P-P!

P, P, P-P-P!

And that's the letter **P**!

MAKE a **P** with two pieces of licorice.

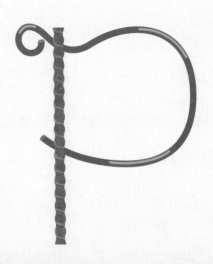

Trace & Sing

TRACE the letter **Q**. START at the green arrow labeled with a number 1.

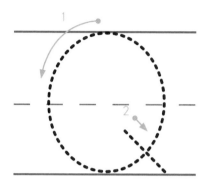

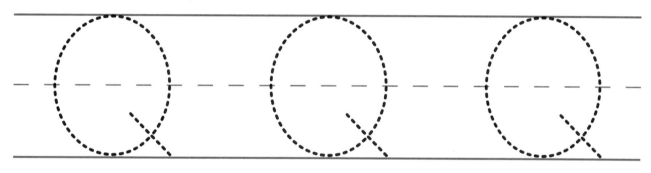

SING this song to the tune of *Wheels on the Bus.*

The letter of the day is

Q-Q-Q, Q-Q-Q, Q-Q-Q!

The letter of the day is

Q-Q-Q,

Today is letter **Q**!

DRAW a **Q**. It's just a circle with a short line crossing near the bottom.

Trace & Sing

TRACE the letter **R**. START at the green arrow labeled with a number 1.

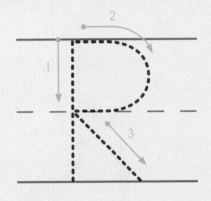

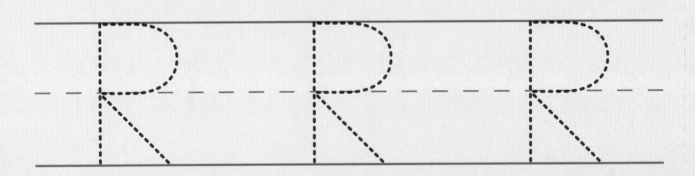

SING this song to the tune of *BINGO*.

MAKE an **R** with ribbon and a ruler.

We learn a letter every day.

Today it's letter **R**!

R, R, R-R-R!

R, R, R-R-R!

R, R, R-R-R!

And that's the letter **R**!

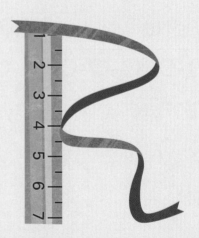

Trace & Sing

TRACE the letter **S**. START at the green arrow labeled with a number 1.

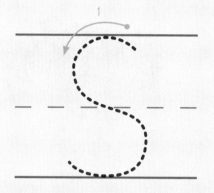

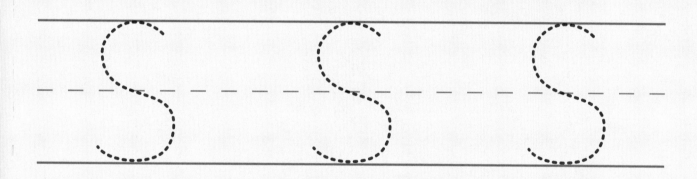

SING this song to the tune of *Wheels on the Bus*.

The letter of the day is

S-S-S, S-S-S, S-S-S!

The letter of the day is

S-S-S,

Today is letter S!

MAKE an **S** out of string.

Trace & Sing

TRACE the letter **T**. START at the green arrow labeled with a number 1.

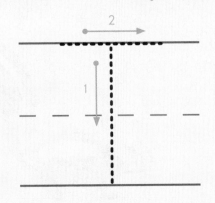

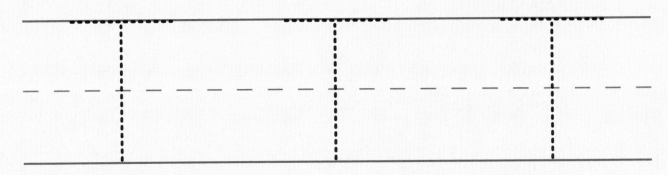

SING this song to the tune of *BINGO*.

We learn a letter every day.

Today it's letter **T**!

T, T, T-T-T!

T, T, T-T-T!

T, T, T-T-T!

And that's the letter **T**!

MAKE a **T** with two twigs (one long and one short).

Trace & Sing

TRACE the letter **U**. START at the green arrow labeled with a number 1.

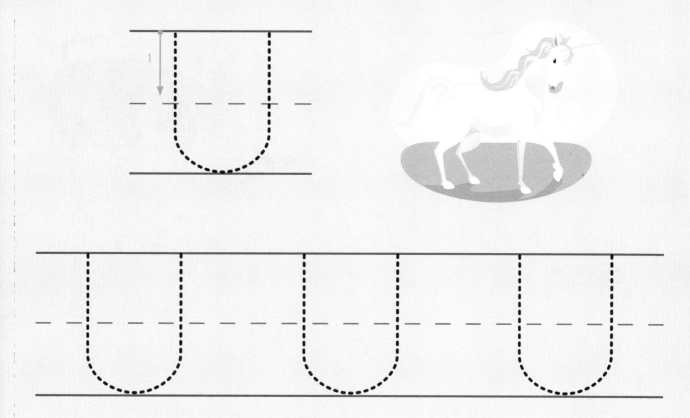

SING this song to the tune of *Wheels on the Bus*.

The letter of the day is
U-U-U, U-U-U, U-U-U!
The letter of the day is
U-U-U,
Today is letter **U!**

MAKE a **U** out of yarn.

The Letter V

Trace & Sing

TRACE the letter **V**. START at the green arrow labeled with a number 1.

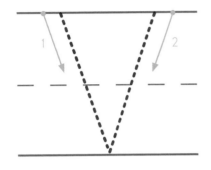

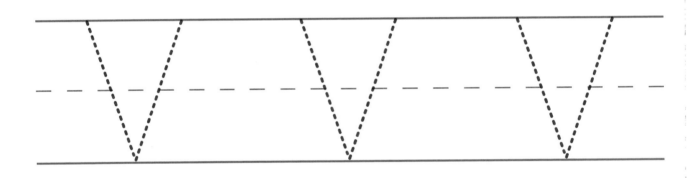

SING this song to the tune of *BINGO*.

We learn a letter every day.

Today it's letter **V**!

V, V, V-V-V!

V, V, V-V-V!

V, V, V-V-V!

And that's the letter **V**!

MAKE a **V** with your fingers.

Trace & Sing

TRACE the letter **W**. START at the green arrow labeled with a number 1.

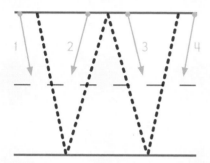

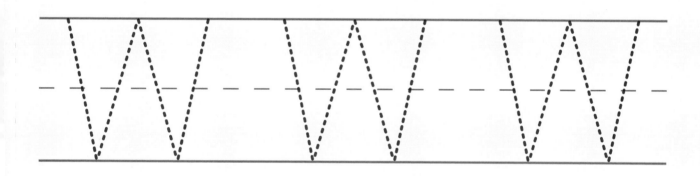

SING this song to the tune of *Wheels on the Bus.*

The letter of the day is
W (dou-ble-you), **W**, **W**!
The letter of the day is **W**,
Today is **W**!

MAKE a **W** using two pairs of jeans.

Trace & Sing

TRACE the letter **X**. START at the green arrow labeled with a number 1.

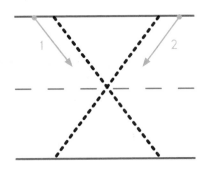

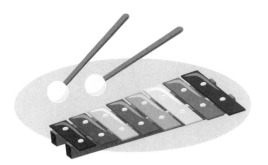

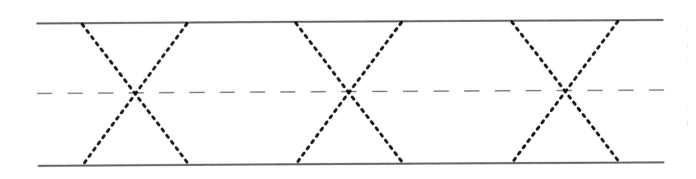

SING this song to the tune of *BINGO*.

We learn a letter every day.

Today it's letter **X**!

X, X, X-X-X!

X, X, X-X-X!

X, X, X-X-X!

And that's the letter **X**!

MAKE an **X** with two carrot sticks.

Trace & Sing

TRACE the letter **Y**. START at the green arrow labeled with a number 1.

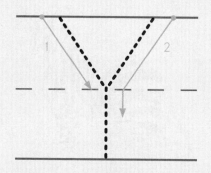

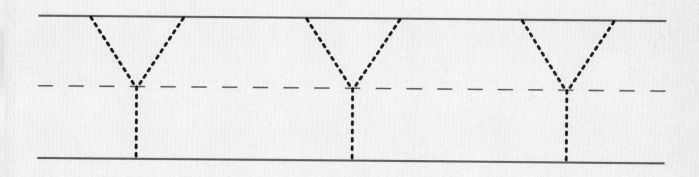

SING this song to the tune of
Wheels on the Bus.

The letter of the day is
Y-Y-Y, Y-Y-Y, Y-Y-Y!
The letter of the day is
Y-Y-Y,
Today is letter Y!

MAKE a **Y** using three crayons.

Trace & Sing

TRACE the letter **Z**. START at the green arrow labeled with a number 1.

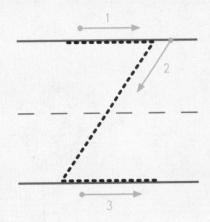

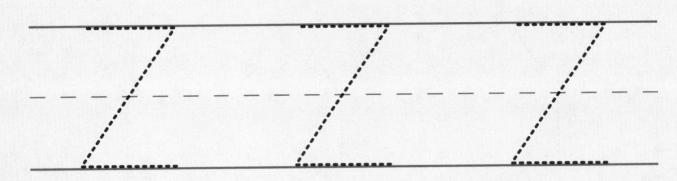

SING this song to the tune of *BINGO.*

We learn a letter every day.

Today it's letter **Z**!

Z, Z, Z-Z-Z!

Z, Z, Z-Z-Z!

Z, Z, Z-Z-Z!

And that's the letter **Z**!

MAKE a **Z** with a piece of dry spaghetti. Break it into one long piece and two short pieces.

Match Maker

SING the alphabet song. FOLLOW ALONG with the alphabet. DRAW a line to connect each letter in the box to its place in the alphabet.

U   K   B   Y   F

A [ ] C D E [ ] G H I

J [ ] L M N O P Q R

S T [ ] V W X [ ] Z

Connect the Dots

DRAW a line to connect the dots in order from **A** to **Z**.

Trace & Sing

You've learned all of the uppercase ABCs! Now it's time for the lowercase abc's. Each uppercase letter has a matching lowercase letter.

Lowercase **a** matches uppercase **A**. TRACE the letter **a**. START at the green arrow labeled with a number 1.

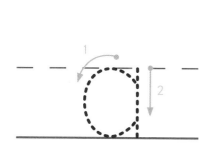

SING this song to the tune of *Jingle Bells*.

MAKE an **a** with two pieces of aluminum foil, twisted up.

Letter **a**! Letter **a**!

Hello, letter **a**!

We meet a letter every day.

Today it's letter **a**!

[Shout] **a**!

Trace & Sing

Lowercase **b** matches uppercase **B**. TRACE the letter **b**.
START at the green arrow labeled with a number 1.

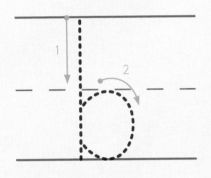

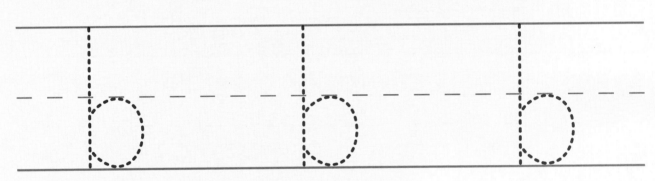

SING this song to the tune of
Mary Had a Little Lamb.

MAKE a **b** using your favorite cereal.

The letter of the day is **b**!

b-b-b!

b-b-b!

The letter of the day is **b**!

Today it's letter **b**!

Trace & Sing

Lowercase **c** matches uppercase **C**. TRACE the letter **c**. START at the green arrow labeled with a number 1.

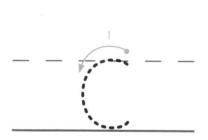

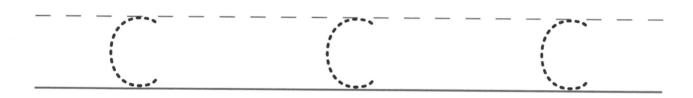

SING this song to the tune of *Jingle Bells*.

DRAW a **c** on the sidewalk with chalk.

Letter **c**! Letter **c**!

Hello, letter **c**!

We meet a letter every day.

Today it's letter **c**!

[Shout] **c**!

Trace & Sing

Lowercase **d** matches uppercase **D**. TRACE the letter **d**.
START at the green arrow labeled with a number 1.

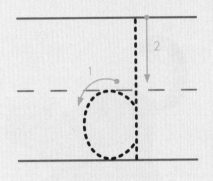

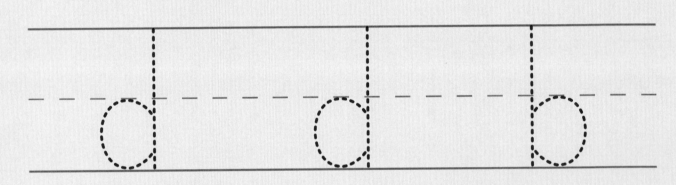

SING this song to the tune of
Mary Had a Little Lamb.

MAKE a **d** using your hands. Hold
your right hand straight, and make
a **c** with the other hand.

The letter of the day is **d**!

d-d-d!

d-d-d!

The letter of the day is **d**!

Today it's letter **d**!

Trace & Sing

Lowercase **e** matches uppercase **E**. TRACE the letter **e**.
START at the green arrow labeled with a number 1.

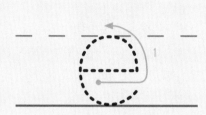

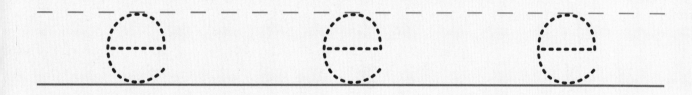

SING this song to the tune of
Jingle Bells.

MAKE an **e** using string.

Letter **e**! Letter **e**!

Hello, letter **e**!

We meet a letter every day.

Today it's letter **e**!

[Shout] **e**!

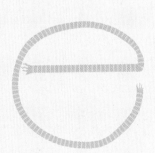

Trace & Sing

Lowercase **f** matches uppercase **F**. TRACE the letter **f**.
START at the green arrow labeled with a number 1.

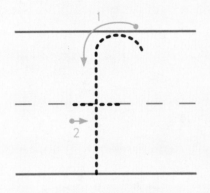

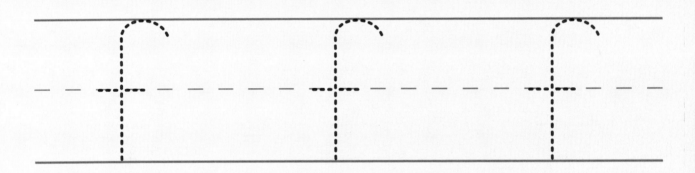

SING this song to the tune of
Mary Had a Little Lamb.

MAKE an **f** using fish crackers.

The letter of the day is **f**!

f-f-f!

f-f-f!

The letter of the day is **f**!

Today it's letter **f**!

Trace & Sing

Lowercase **g** matches uppercase **G**. TRACE the letter **g**. START at the green arrow labeled with a number 1.

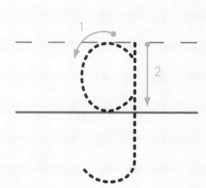

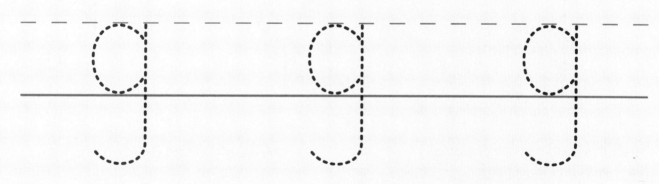

SING this song to the tune of *Jingle Bells*.

MAKE a **g** using grapes.

Letter **g**! Letter **g**!

Hello, letter **g**!

We meet a letter every day.

Today it's letter **g**!

[Shout] **g**!

The Letter h

Trace & Sing

Lowercase **h** matches uppercase **H**. TRACE the letter **h**.
START at the green arrow labeled with a number 1.

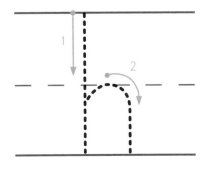

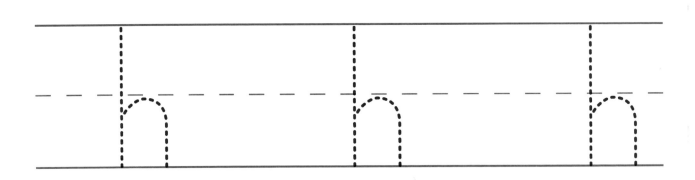

SING this song to the tune of *Mary Had a Little Lamb*.

MAKE an **h** using a ruler and a sock.

The letter of the day is **h**!

h-**h**-**h**!

h-**h**-**h**!

The letter of the day is **h**!

Today it's letter **h**!

I i

Trace & Sing

Lowercase **i** matches uppercase **I**. TRACE the letter **i**.
START at the green arrow labeled with a number 1.

SING this song to the tune of
Jingle Bells.

MAKE an **i** using a baby carrot and a grape.

Letter **i**! Letter **i**!

Hello, letter **i**!

We meet a letter every day.

Today it's letter **i**!

[Shout] **i**!

Trace & Sing

Lowercase **j** matches uppercase **J**. TRACE the letter **j**.
START at the green arrow labeled with a number 1.

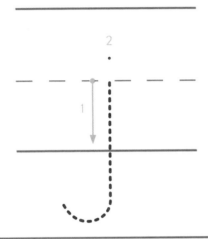

SING this song to the tune of
Mary Had a Little Lamb.

MAKE a **j** using jellybeans.

The letter of the day is **j**!

j-j-j!

j-j-j!

The letter of the day is **j**!

Today it's letter **j**!

Trace & Sing

Lowercase **k** matches uppercase **K**. TRACE the letter **k**.
START at the green arrow labeled with a number 1.

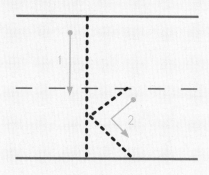

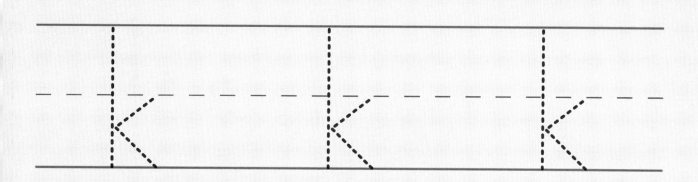

SING this song to the tune of
Jingle Bells.

Letter k! Letter k!

Hello, letter k!

We meet a letter every day.

Today it's letter k!

[Shout] k!

MAKE a **k** using three pieces of chalk
(one long and two short).

The Letter l

Trace & Sing

Lowercase **l** matches uppercase **L**. TRACE the letter **l**.
START at the green arrow labeled with a number 1.

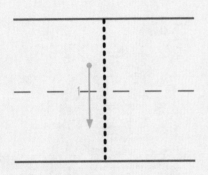

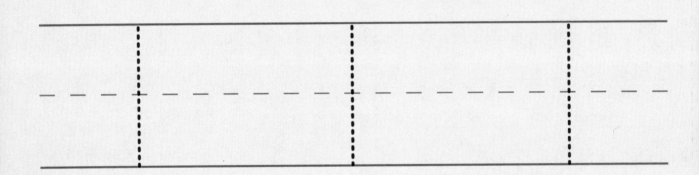

SING this song to the tune of
Mary Had a Little Lamb.

The letter of the day is l!

l-l-l!

l-l-l!

The letter of the day is l!

Today it's letter l!

DRAW an **l** with your largest crayon. It's just a straight line!

Trace & Sing

Lowercase **m** matches uppercase **M**. TRACE the letter **m**.
START at the green arrow labeled with a number 1.

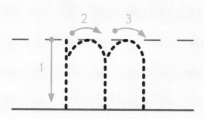

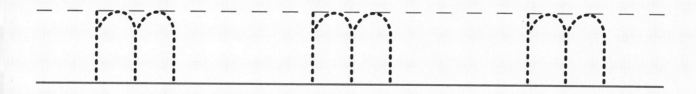

SING this song to the tune of
Jingle Bells.

MAKE an **m** using beads.

Letter **m**! Letter **m**!

Hello, letter **m**!

We meet a letter every day.

Today it's letter **m**!

[Shout] **m**!

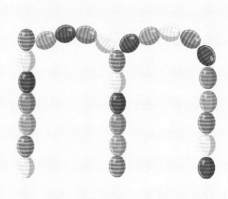

The Letter n

Trace & Sing

Lowercase **n** matches uppercase **N**. TRACE the letter **n**.
START at the green arrow labeled with a number 1.

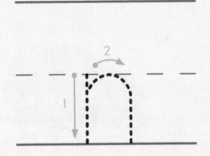

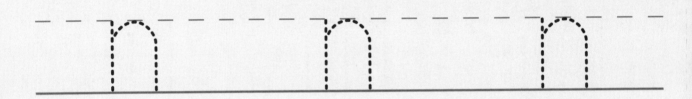

SING this song to the tune of
Mary Had a Little Lamb.

MAKE an **n** using two pieces of
spaghetti (one wet and one dry).

The letter of the day is **n**!

n-n-n!

n-n-n!

The letter of the day is **n**!

Today it's letter **n**!

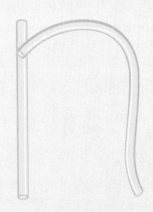

Trace & Sing

Lowercase **o** matches uppercase **O**. TRACE the letter **o**. START at the green arrow labeled with a number 1.

SING this song to the tune of *Jingle Bells.*

MAKE an **o** with your hand.

Letter **o**! Letter **o**!

Hello, letter **o**!

We meet a letter every day.

Today it's letter **o**!

[Shout] **o**!

Trace & Sing

Lowercase **p** matches uppercase **P**. TRACE the letter **p**.
START at the green arrow labeled with a number 1.

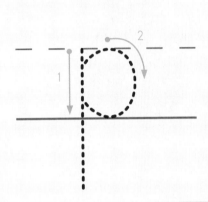

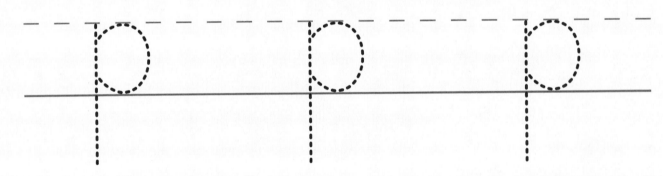

SING this song to the tune of
Mary Had a Little Lamb.

MAKE a **p** using two pillowcases.
(Take out the pillows.)

The letter of the day is **p**!

p-p-p!

p-p-p!

The letter of the day is **p**!

Today it's letter **p**!

Trace & Sing

Lowercase **q** matches uppercase **Q**. TRACE the letter **q**. START at the green arrow labeled with a number 1.

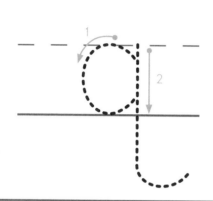

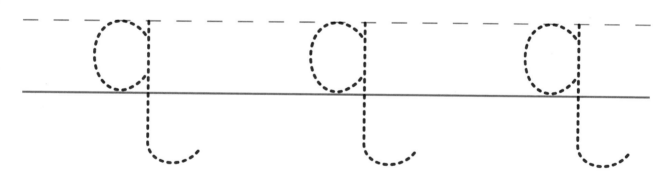

SING this song to the tune of *Jingle Bells*.

MAKE a **q** using quarters.

Letter **q**! Letter **q**!

Hello, letter **q**!

We meet a letter every day.

Today it's letter **q**!

[Shout] **q**!

The Letter r

Trace & Sing

Lowercase **r** matches uppercase **R**. TRACE the letter **r**.
START at the green arrow labeled with a number 1.

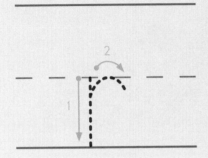

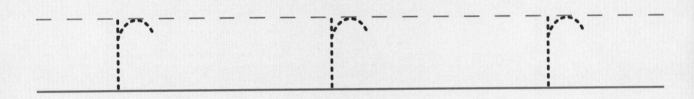

SING this song to the tune of
Mary Had a Little Lamb.

MAKE an **r** using rocks.

The letter of the day is r!

r-r-r!

r-r-r!

The letter of the day is r!

Today it's letter r!

Trace & Sing

Lowercase **s** matches uppercase **S**. TRACE the letter **s**.
START at the green arrow labeled with a number 1.

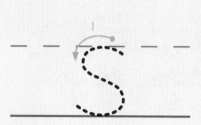

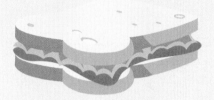

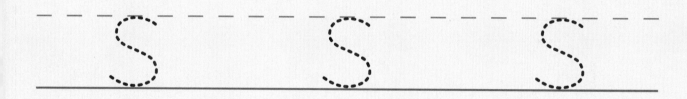

SING this song to the tune of
Jingle Bells.

MAKE an **s** using a shoelace.

Letter **s**! Letter **s**!

Hello, letter **s**!

We meet a letter every day.

Today it's letter **s**!

[Shout] **s**!

49

The Letter t

Trace & Sing

Lowercase **t** matches uppercase **T**. TRACE the letter **t**.
START at the green arrow labeled with a number 1.

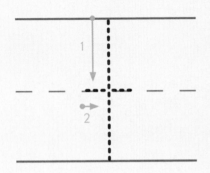

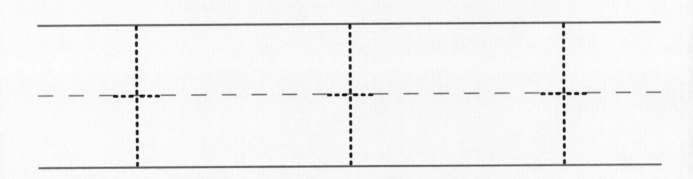

SING this song to the tune of
Mary Had a Little Lamb.

MAKE a **t** using two ties.

The letter of the day is **t**!

t-t-t!

t-t-t!

The letter of the day is **t**!

Today it's letter **t**!

Trace & Sing

Lowercase **u** matches uppercase **U**. TRACE the letter **u**. START at the green arrow labeled with a number 1.

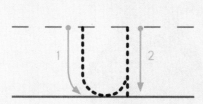

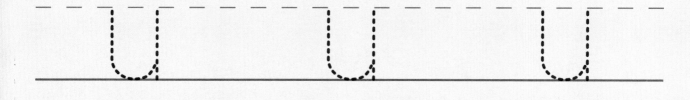

SING this song to the tune of *Jingle Bells.*

MAKE a **u** using two pieces of spaghetti (one wet and one dry).

Letter **u**! Letter **u**!

Hello, letter **u**!

We meet a letter every day.

Today it's letter **u**!

[Shout] **u**!

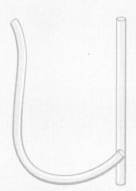

The Letter v

Trace & Sing

Lowercase **v** matches uppercase **V**. TRACE the letter **v**. START at the green arrow labeled with a number 1.

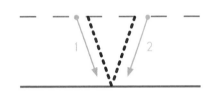

SING this song to the tune of *Mary Had a Little Lamb.*

The letter of the day is **v**!

v-v-v!

v-v-v!

The letter of the day is **v**!

Today it's letter **v**!

DRAW a **v** using a violet crayon. It's just two short lines that meet at the bottom.

Trace & Sing

Lowercase **w** matches uppercase **W**. TRACE the letter **w**. START at the green arrow labeled with a number 1.

SING this song to the tune of *Jingle Bells*.

It's **w**, **w**!

Hello, letter **w**!

We meet a letter every day.

Today it's **w**!

[Shout] **w**!

MAKE a **w** using four markers.

Trace & Sing

Lowercase **x** matches uppercase **X**. TRACE the letter **x**.
START at the green arrow labeled with a number 1.

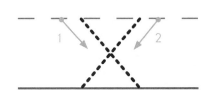

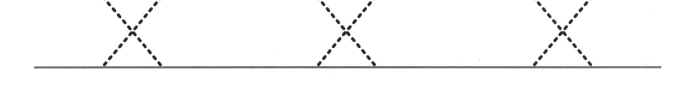

SING this song to the tune of
Mary Had a Little Lamb.

MAKE an **x** with your arms.
Shout "X marks the spot!"

The letter of the day is **x**!

x-x-x!

x-x-x!

The letter of the day is **x**!

Today it's letter **x**!

Trace & Sing

Lowercase **y** matches uppercase **Y**. TRACE the letter **y**.
START at the green arrow labeled with a number 1.

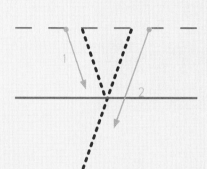

SING this song to the tune of
Jingle Bells.

Letter y! Letter y!

Hello, letter y!

We meet a letter every day.

Today it's letter y!

[Shout] y!

MAKE a **y** using two socks
(one small and one big).

Trace & Sing

Lowercase **z** matches uppercase **Z**. TRACE the letter **z**.
START at the green arrow labeled with a number 1.

Zz

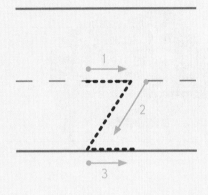

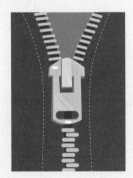

SING this song to the tune of
Mary Had a Little Lamb.

MAKE a **z** with three strips of
paper (all the same size).

The letter of the day is **z**!

z-z-z!

z-z-z!

The letter of the day is **z**!

Today it's letter **z**!

Match Maker

DRAW a line to connect each pair of uppercase and lowercase letters.

a   F

b   E

c   G

d   A

e   D

f   C

g   B

Match Maker

DRAW a line to connect each pair of uppercase and lowercase letters.

h   L

i   I

j   N

k   J

l   K

m   H

n   M

Connect the Dots

DRAW a line to connect the dots in order from **a** to **z**.

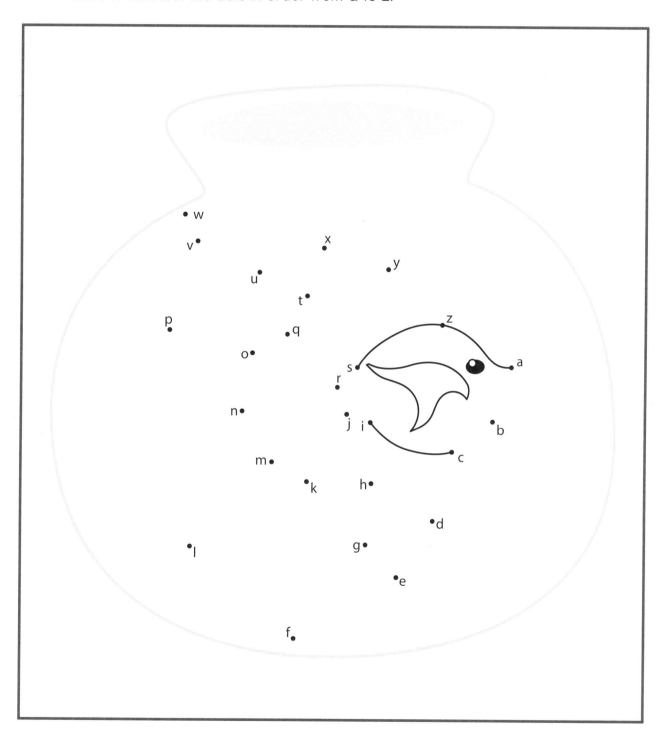

Match Maker

SING the alphabet song. FOLLOW ALONG with the alphabet. DRAW a line to connect each letter in the box to its place in the alphabet.

z   l   d   q   w

a   b   c   ☐   e   f   g   h   i

j   k   ☐   m   n   o   p   ☐   r

s   t   u   v   ☐   x   y   ☐

Check out Sylvan's complete line of offerings!

SINGLE-SUBJECT WORKBOOKS

☑ Pre-K–5th grade

☑ Focus on individual skills and subjects

☑ Fun activities and exercises

3-IN-1 SUPER WORKBOOKS

☑ Pre-K–5th grade

☑ Three Sylvan single-subject workbooks in one package

☑ Perfect practice for the student who needs to focus on a range of topics

A $39 value for just $18.99!

FUN ON THE RUN ACTIVITY BOOKS

☑ Kindergarten–2nd grade

☑ Just $3.99/$4.75 Can.

☑ Colorful games and activities for on-the-go learning

FLASHCARD SETS

☑ Spelling for Kindergarten–2nd grade

☑ Vocabulary for 3rd–5th grade

☑ Includes 230 words to help students reinforce skills

PAGE PER DAY WORKBOOKS

☑ Pre-K–1st grade

☑ Perforated pages—perfect for your child to do just one workbook page each day

☑ Extra practice the easy way!

Try FREE pages today at SylvanPagePerDay.com

With just a **PAGE PER DAY**, your child gets extra practice ... the easy way! Get sample pages for free!

Whether the goal is to get a jumpstart on new material or to brush up on past lessons, setting aside a small amount of time each day to complete one Sylvan workbook page will help your child review and improve skills, grow self-confidence, and develop a love of learning.

Visit SylvanPagePerDay.com to get free workbook printables in the grade of your choice!

✂ CUT ALONG THE DOTTED LINE